FUN FACTS

Ripley's Believe It or Not!®

Kids

& SILLY STORIES

Editor Jessica Firpi
Designers Patti Moliver, Jordie Rutledge, Penny Stamp
Reprographics *POST LLC

ISBN 978-1-60991-167-6 (US)

Library of Congress Control Number: 2016941899

For information regarding permission, write to
VP Intellectual Property
Ripley Entertainment Inc.
Suite 188, 7576 Kingspointe Parkway
Orlando, Florida, 32819
Email: publishing@ripleys.com
www.ripleybooks.com

Manufactured in China
in June/2016
1st printing

PUBLISHER'S NOTE
While every effort has been made to verify the accuracy
of the entries in this book, the Publishers cannot be held
responsible for any errors contained in the work. They
would be glad to receive any information from readers.

WARNING
Some of the stunts and activities in this book are undertaken
by experts and should not be attempted by anyone without
adequate training and supervision.

a Jim Pattison Company

FUN FACTS

Ripley's Believe It or Not!

Kids

& SILLY STORIES

5

All CLOWNFISH are born male.

Leaf-eating African colobus monkeys

Excuse me!

often **burp** in each other's faces.

Norway introduced **salmon sushi** to Japan!

Maryland's official state sport is **JOUSTING.**

Traffic today in central London moves at the same speed as horse-drawn carriages once did.

Spiders can walk on and breathe under water.

Put 'em up!

Male Koalas RAISE THEIR VOICES to avoid a fight.

Engineer Lance Abernethy created the world's smallest working drill and saw with a 3-D printer.

Both are smaller than a US quarter!

Artist Erin Bonilla and guinea pig breeder Heather Beebe did an adorable photo shoot

scrub-a-dub-dub!

of hairless guinea pig **STRAWBERRY SHORTCAKE** taking a bubble bath!

$$1111 \times 1111 = 1234321$$

$$11111 \times 11111 = 123454321$$

$$111111 \times 111111 = 12345654321$$

$$1111111 \times 1111111 = 1234567654321$$

Pterodactyls, and other "flying dinosaurs," are not really dinosaurs.

Just as some people talk in their sleep, sign language speakers sometimes sign in their sleep.

Unlike many spider species, tarantulas do NOT spin webs to catch their prey.

STOMACH FACTS

Stomach rumbling can happen at any time, not just when you're hungry.

Seahorses, lungfish, and platypuses have no stomachs!

Even if you eat while hanging upside down, the food will still get to your stomach.

There are **MORE BIKES THAN PEOPLE** in Amsterdam, the Netherlands.

Spiders, lobsters, and snails have **BLUE BLOOD** due to the presence of hemocyanin, which contains copper.

The metal part on a pencil is called a **ferrule.**

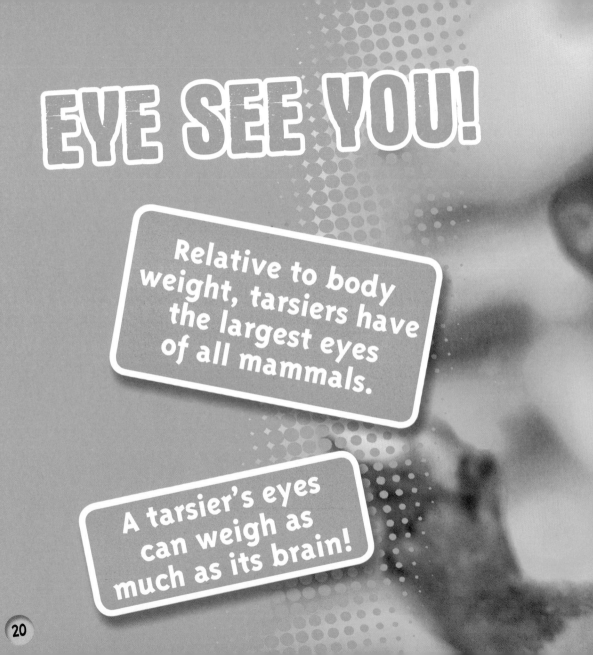

EYE SEE YOU!

Relative to body weight, tarsiers have the largest eyes of all mammals.

A tarsier's eyes can weigh as much as its brain!

This *hymenopus coronatus* (otherwise known as the orchid or walking flower mantis)

mimics an orchid to hide itself from predators.

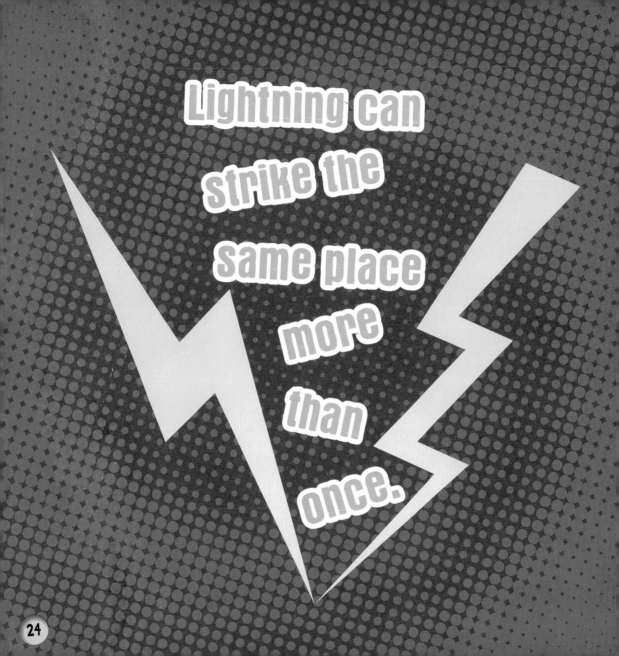

Lightning can strike the same place more than once.

In 1954, a goat named **SMELLY** was elected to a city council in Brazil.

Fish cough.

cough, cough

Harry Potter® characters Sirius Black and Bellatrix Lestrange were named after stars.

Full moons appear **BRIGHTER** in winter than in summer.

NASA's Hubble Space Telescope weighs as much as two adult elephants!

A family of lions caused a little traffic jam in Central Kruger Park, South Africa, when they took a stroll along a main road.

A palm tree is not a tree— it's more closely related to grass.

Some hummingbirds hold their tiny nests together using silk stolen from spiderwebs.

Japan's highest mountain, Mount Fuji, has free Wi-Fi!

An
OCTOPUS
has
six arms and two legs—
not eight arms.

Earth, Texas, is the only place on Earth named "Earth."

No one has ever seen a giraffe swim.

HALLOWEEN CRABS

Halloween crabs spend most of their time on land, but they must return to the water to lay eggs.

Halloween crabs are also called moon crabs!

A whale's earwax can be as thick as a mattress.

There is a salamander nicknamed the SNOT OTTER.

Crows are
so smart they can
play pranks on
each other and on
other animals!

Photographer Vyacheslav Mischenko captured this amazing image of a snail looking at its reflection near his home in the Ukraine.

Phil Ferguson, aka Chili Philly, started crotcheting funny hats and sharing them on Instagram to make friends when he moved to Australia!

I'm so hungry!

40

I'm a fungi, nice to meet you.

A new species of fungus named geastrum britannicum look just like little HUMANS.

At a training academy in the United Kingdom, ship captains practice on mini versions of the world's biggest ships!

This rebellious KINGFISHER didn't mind breaking the rules when it came time for a meal.

Kon'nichiwa

Godzilla is an official citizen of Japan.

The United States has more Spanish-speaking people than Spain.

Vikings never wore helmets with horns.

Despite its looks, this little creature is completely harmless. It is a **common nawab caterpillar** found in South Asia.

This wacky work of art called "Pick Yourself Up and Pull Yourself Together"

was designed by Alex Chinneck and displayed in London.

In 2016,
a man set a record for
Most Peeps® Eaten
in 15 minutes.

He ate
200 PEEPS.

The Brontosaurus never existed.

A light year does not measure time— it measures distance.

Barry the Bedlington terrier first dazzled the Internet by riding a tricycle, but he soon upgraded to a Rolls-Royce.

Beep Beep!

Mmmm...

Homer Pugalicious, an adorable pug from Perth, Australia, loves food and naps.

Follow Homer on Instagram or Facebook!

53

A group of jellies is called a **SMACK.**

In 1971, astronaut Alan Shepard played golf on the Moon with this golf ball.

FIRST GOLF BALL

ON THE MOON

FEB. 6, 1971

Native to New Zealand and Australia, Clathrus archeri fungus is also known as

DEVIL'S FINGERS.

ALERT ALL CRAYONS

Using old dental tools, Hoang Tran, from Sunnyvale, California, carves characters from films and books into the tips of crayons.

Check out these *Star Wars*® characters!

Scarlet macaws eat clay from riverbanks— and no one is sure why.

In Finland, when a student earns their PhD, they are given a top hat and a sword.

HEDGEHOG FACTS

Hedgehog spikes are not barbed and not poisonous.

A political party once tried to get a hedgehog elected to parliament in New Zealand!

There used to be the International Hedgehog Olympic Games (IHOG).

A baby hedgehog is called a "piglet."

63

Artist **Jim Bachor** fills in potholes with fun mosaic art pieces.

He was inspired when he saw ancient mosaics while on a dig in Pompeii, Italy.

Bats are true hibernators, meaning they're in such a deep sleep they appear dead.

Brazil once tried to sell an

AIRCRAFT CARRIER

on eBay®.

Most fish have taste buds all over their body.

Hmm...
Needs more
salt!

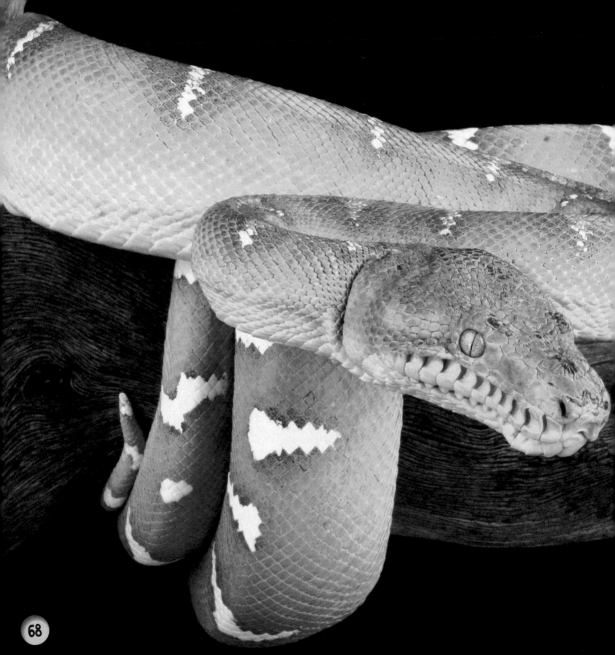

You can't esssssscape me!

Emerald green tree boas have been known to grab birds in mid-flight!

69

Florida
has more
lightning strikes
than any
other US state.

A group of bears

I'm the real sloth.

is called a sloth.

BUZZ FEED

A honeybee visits 50–100 flowers during one collection trip.

Bees need about 2 million flowers to make one pound (0.45 kg) of honey.

A hive of bees flies over 55,000 miles (88,514 km) to bring you one pound (0.45 kg) of honey.

The only bees that die after they sting you are honeybees.

The Chinese were the first to create paper money.

In Aspen, Colorado, you're not allowed to throw **snowballs.**

Strawberries, blackberries, and raspberries are technically not berries.

Danishes are from Austria, not from Denmark.

You can't catch warts from toads, but you can catch warts from other people.

Keep those people away from me!

ICEBERGS

are made of freshwater— not salt water.

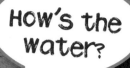

COOLING

A bold group of **vervet monkeys** in South Africa snuck into a family's backyard to have a pool party.

OFF

GLASS is neither liquid nor solid.

You can buy bacon-flavored toothpaste.

If touched by a human, birds will **NOT** abandon their babies.

Mama, Mama, Mama...

81

Even when dead,
a jelly's venomous
tentacles can still sting.

Basset hounds have the second best sense of smell of all breeds.

Their long ears help sweep the scent up toward their nose.

A youth organization known as

GERMEN CREW

joined the Mexican government to paint

OVER 209 HOUSES

on a hillside town in Mexico.

Belgium is home to the world's first **FRENCH FRY MUSEUM.**

The little piece of plastic on the end of your shoelace is called an

AGLET.

Velvet ants are actually

WASPS!

The electric toaster was invented decades before pre-sliced bread.

In Kentucky, there's a town called "MONKEYS EYEBROW."

Babies are born
COLOR-BLIND.

Green basilisk lizards

A 4 inch (10 cm) high LEGO® figure of Britain's Queen Elizabeth II had a real diamond-encrusted crown!

FRIENDLY PASTURES

Lee Kwang-ho fills his coffee shop in Seoul, South Korea, with sheep! He borrows sheep from a local farm and lets them roam around his café.

Tennessee has a full-scale replica of the **PARTHENON,** an ancient Greek temple.

Charles Fisher from Nottinghamshire, England, made a replica of

Thomas the Tank Engine

from a

hedge.

As if out of a fairy tale, a brown bear named Stepan had a picnic with a little girl and her mother in Moscow, Russia.

The Incas measured time by how long it took for potatoes to cook.

MAINE
is the only US state with a one-syllable name.

You have taste buds in your throat.

The mimic octopus can impersonate up to 15 marine species, including sea snakes, stingrays, lionfish, and jellies.

Although it can fly, the long-legged secretary bird is one of only two bird species that hunts on foot.

Can you spot the sheep?

Canadian farmer Liezel Kennedy
almost couldn't find
her flock of 550 sheep
against the snowy landscape.

*Hint: Look between the grass and snow.

Did you know that
TUG-OF-WAR
was an Olympic sport
between 1900 and 1920?

The first Pilgrims in America would not have eaten potatoes at the time because Europeans believed they were

POISONOUS.

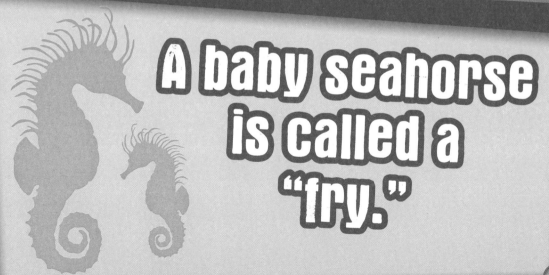

A baby seahorse is called a "fry."

These funny foxes were super photogenic when they got their paws on a photographer's camera in Danube-Auen National Park in Austria.

Ailurophobia

is the extreme fear of cats.

It can take 10 years for a saguaro cactus to grow just one inch (2.5 cm).

August 16 is National Tell a Joke Day!

Eating ice cream makes your temperature RISE.

Ripley's senior researcher Sabrina has a dog named Cruella that is

ALLERGIC TO HUMANS!

She's now much happier wearing her Lycra® suit.

America's first air force included hot-air balloons.

Stars do not TWINKLE.

Billboards are illegal in Hawaii

There is a scholarship available only for **paintballers.**

You cannot see the Great Wall of China from space.

An art teacher in Wyoming creates **chalkboard drawings** to inspire his students!

119

Raindrops aren't really shaped like drops—they start out perfectly round and then become more like the top half of a hamburger bun!

Supai, Arizona, in the Grand Canyon is the only place in the US where mail is still delivered via mule.

Mail time!

A hyacinth macaw's beak is so powerful it can even

CRACK COCONUTS!

HORSING AROUND

Kentucky Derby racehorses always walk to the starting gate with their BFF.

Horses with pink skin can get a sunburn.

Horses see better at night than humans.

Rescued lambs at Edgar's Mission Farm Sanctuary in Victoria, Australia, wear colorful sweaters to keep warm during the chilly winter months.

I'm nice and warm. Are ewe?

PEEK-A-BOO!

In South Africa, nature guide Rudi Hulshof took this perfectly timed photo of TWO GIRAFFES! Although it looks like one animal, there are actually two giraffes with one poking its head out of the bush.

Artist Iantha Naicker from South Africa paints intricate scenes on her left palm—but then washes them away!

Chinese fortune cookies were invented in San Francisco, California.

Late-night dancing was illegal in Japan until 2015!

Killer whales are not just whales—they are also the largest member of the dolphin species.

With the help of her owner John, **BAILEY** the golden retriever poses doing everyday actvities.

Check out this cute Thanksgiving photo of Bailey posing six different times!

Termites pick the wood they eat based on how it sounds when chewed.

Peanuts aren't nuts, but they are related to peas.

Despite their names, **WHITE** and **BLACK** rhinos are both actually GRAY.

To raise money for charity, **IKEA**® turned children's drawings into real plush toys.

The strawberry poison-dart frog is also called the blue-jeans frog...

I wonder why...

These frogs also chirp like a bird!

The Emperor tamarin was named after its elegant white mustache, which resembles the one a German emperor once had.

I mustache you a question...

Trees cannot grow higher than about

453 feet

(138 m)

because they can't pull water any higher up their trunks.

For centuries, Italian banks held on to cheese in exchange for good rates on loans—and some banks still do!

Producing three to seven different fruits, fruit salad trees actually exist!

California's official state animal is extinct.

CALIFORNIA REPUBLIC

During a stealth hunting mission, a Northern hawk owl stared intently at the camera while flying just like a torpedo!

TORPEDO

The wide-eyed bird is native to Finland and is one of the few owl species that are only active during the day.

I'm coming to get you!

OWL

The tiny Honduran white bat
is also known as the
MARSHMALLOW BAT!

To promote a new Bugs Bunny TV show, a few squirrels were spotted wearing little capes and running around a London park.

Canadian mom Ruth Oosterman creates beautiful drawings with her toddler Eve.

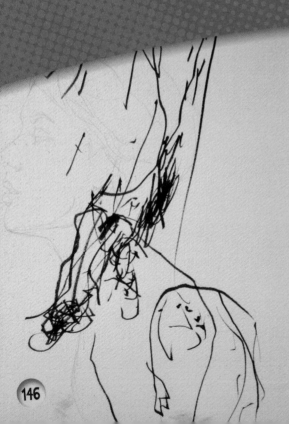

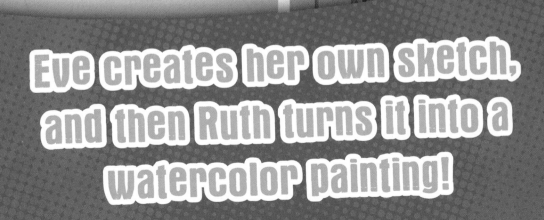

Eve creates her own sketch, and then Ruth turns it into a watercolor painting!

Dartmouth College in New Hampshire is older than the United States!

In 1950, the first TV remote control was called "Lazy Bones."

Manta rays sometimes LAUNCH

THEMSELVES

out of the sea,
a behavior known
as breaching.

FAMILY FUN

The Zenz family created friendly street art by painting rocks, sticks, and leaves

and then leaving them
all over town for people to find!

The three-banded armadillo is the only species of armadillo that can roll up into a ball for safety.

China joined its five time zones into one— so the sunrise can be as late as 10 am!

Pirates did not have people walk the plank.

Check out the newest exhibits from the Ripley's warehouse!

Here's a motorcyle made from recycled Coca-Cola® cans.

Artist Eric Shupe created this horse sculpture out of spoons!

In Sweden, the passengers body heat in Stockholm Central Railway Station is used to heat a nearby building.

An Olympic wrestling match once lasted 11 hours.

When you run, there is a point when both your feet are off the ground.

There are more historical artifacts **in the ocean** than in all of the world's museums combined!

If you visit the Cincinnati Main Library, be sure to see this book fountain!

King crabs aren't crabs.

But I feel crabby.

Morton's toe is when your second toe

is LONGER than your big toe.

Women have longer intestines than men.

No one really knows what "Nintendo" means.

Antarctica is the only continent without a time zone.

Maybe we are frozen in time.

A mosquito bite bump is caused by its saliva.

The *Hydnellum peckii* fungus secretes red drops that look like blood.

American artist Meredith Yarborough has knitted

Paw-sitive cat-itude!

over 200 charming costumes for her pet cat, Bullwinkle!

OCTO-POTS

This shiny, metal octopus was made using pots, pans, and spoons in Shanghai, China.

蜕变

www.fissler.c
www.fissleraci
400-608-8689

A restaurant in France sold Darth Vader burgers

You want fries with that?

with buns that were dyed black.

You don't have to say hi every time you swim past me.

Goldfish have a memory of a few months—not a few seconds.

Crossing your arms can reduce pain by confusing your brain.

Darius the rabbit measures over 4 ft. long (1.2 m) and weighs a whopping **50 lbs (22.7 kg)**, while his son Jeff is already 3 ft. 8 in. (1.12 m) long!

This giant rabbit family eats their way through:

- a huge dog bowl full of specialist rabbit food every day

- one bale of hay a week

- 2,000 carrots and 700 apples a year

Artist Carla Pires de Carvalho Fernandes designed this brain-shaped public phone booth!

It was installed in Sao Paulo, Brazil, in 2012.

Swarley the prairie dog is best friends with Lil Sebastian the goat! Lil Sebastian even lets Swarley ride piggyback.

Photographer Geert Weggen specializes in taking amazing photos of

SQUIRRELS!

GHOST ANTS
have SEE-THROUGH stomachs.

Not all ladybugs have **SPOTS**—some are **STRIPED**, **CHECKERED**, or have no pattern at all!

Did you know that Donald Duck's middle name is **Fauntleroy?**

Sculptor John Lopez builds works of art with scrap metal!

Check out that vibrant blue peacock and this "Colt of Many Colors"!

THE HUNT RANCH

For the **450th ANNIVERSARY** of the Brazilian city of Rio de Janeiro, people helped themselves to a **450 meter (1,476 ft) long cake!**

Electric eels can deliver an electric shock **so powerful** it can drop a horse to the ground!

I'm not horsing around!

Believe it or not, there's a world record for most feet and armpits **sniffed.**

The scientific term for "brain freeze" is sphenopalatine ganglioneuralgia.

Bubble gum is pink because when it was invented, that was the only food dye color on hand.

Ninety-four percent of life on Earth

is aquatic.

Before the dwarf planet "Makemake" was offically named, scientists called it "Easterbunny."

CHEETAH FACTS

Cheetahs have no claw sheaths, so their claws always stick out.

When running, cheetahs use their tails to help them steer and keep their balance, like the rudder of a boat.

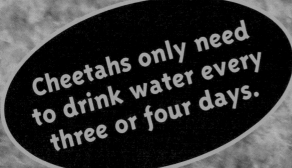

Artist Steve Casino paints tiny versions of celebrities

ON PEANUTS!

Early baseballs were sometimes made of **fish eyes** covered in leather.

Smelling the herb **ROSEMARY** can improve your memory.

The **100 pleats** on a chef's hat are said to represent all the ways you can cook an

EGG.

You can take "The Joy of Garbage" college course at Santa Clara University.

In 1998,
Topeka, Kansas,
renamed itself
"ToPikachu"
for one day.

Some
piranhas
are
vegetarians!

Surprising their keepers, some common **SQUIRREL MONKEYS** made friends with a few **CAPYBARAS*** at a zoo in the Netherlands.

*Capybaras are from South America, and they're the largest rodent in the world!

Picking up seaweed
on the beach at night is

ILLEGAL

in New Hampshire.

"Oh, Look, a Chicken!"

is a real college course at Belmont University in Tennessee.

EGYPTIANS
invented the first breath mints.

Photographer Ian Thomas waited four hours in freezing temperatures at Dudley Zoo in England to finally catch a tiger rolling a

HUGE SNOWBALL!

ARE YOU LOST?

In January 2016, the Transit Commission of Ecuador stumbled upon an adorable sloth clinging to a pole along a highway. After a visit to the veterinarian, the happy sloth was returned to its natural habitat.

Meerkats will eat deadly scorpions... stingers and all!

Yikes!

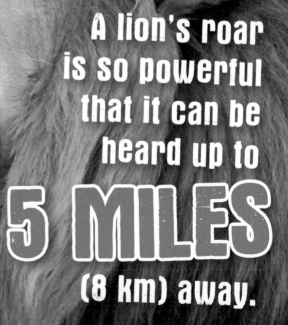

How's my breath?

A lion's roar is so powerful that it can be heard up to

5 MILES

(8 km) away.

Believe it or not, the longest mountain range in the world is underwater.

The hyoid bone is the only bone in the human body not connected to another bone.

Tiger urine can smell like POPCORN!

The dot over an

"i" or "j"

is called a tittle.

Pulling your foot from quicksand requires about the same amount of force as lifting a car.

a frilled shark eat.

North Dakota tried to drop the "North" from its name—twice!

A single dandelion can produce 2,000 seeds!

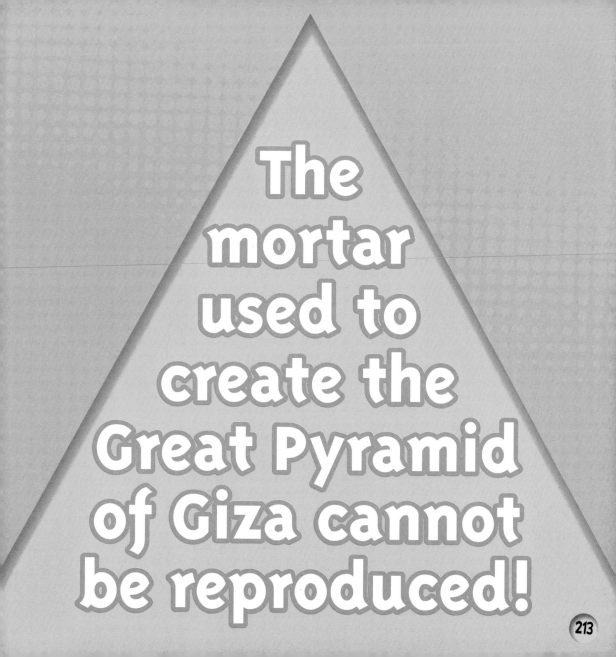

The mortar used to create the Great Pyramid of Giza cannot be reproduced!

213

The underside of a horse's hoof is called a frog!

A tiny village in India is known as the "Chess Village" because every villager plays the game!

In 2015, a record 98 shark attacks occurred worldwide (59 happened in the US).

One **BARBIE® DOLL** is sold about every 3 seconds.

You can't sell your eye in Texas.

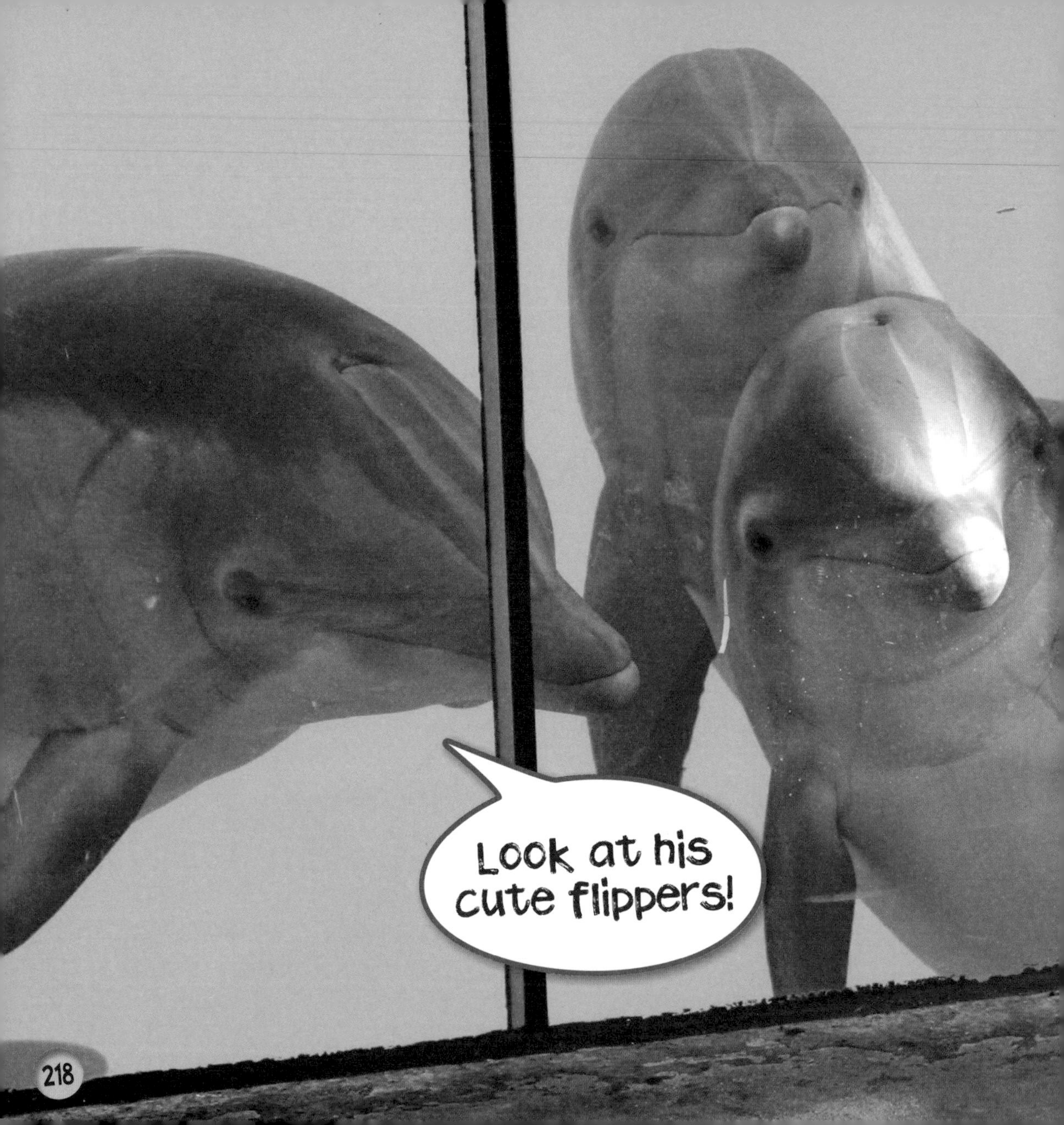
Look at his cute flippers!

When **FOZZIE** the African penguin walked past their enclosure, four curious dolphins had to check him out!

INDEX

PHOTO CREDITS